D1444497

COOKIE INDULGENCE

150 Easy Cookie Recipes

BONNIE SCOTT

ISBN-13: 978-1479382637

150 Easy Cookie Recipes   I
Cookie Indulgence: 150 Easy Cookie Recipes   9
Use the Best Quality, Appropriate Ingredients   10
How You Combine Your Ingredients Makes a Difference   10
Use the Proper Equipment for Better Cookies   11
Cookie Baking Accessories and Tools   12
Bakery Style Cookies   13
The Best Cookie Gifts from Your Kitchen   14

CHOCOLATE CHIP COOKIES   17

Double Chocolate Walnut Drops   17
Chocolate Pudding Cookies   18
Cookie Brittle   19
Excellent Chocolate Chip Cookies   20
All-In-One Cookie   21
Chocolate Krinkle Cookies   22
Honey Chocolate Chip Cookies   23
Pumpkin Chip Cookies   24
Dolittle Cookies   25
Bakery Chocolate Chip Cookies   26
Deluxe Chocolate Chip Cookies   27
Zucchini Chocolate Chip Cookies   28

OATMEAL COOKIES   30

Apple Oatmeal Cookies   30
Coffee Shop Oatmeal Cookies   31
Pioneer Cornflake Cookies   32
Cracker Jack Cookies   33
Oatmeal Gem Cookies   34
Moist Oatmeal Cookies   35
Double Chocolate Oatmeal Cookies   36
Oatmeal Raisin Cookies   37
Chocolate Chip Oatmeal Cookies   38

CHERRY OATMEAL COOKIES 39
SKINNY OATMEAL COOKIES 40

FRUIT COOKIES 42

BANANA CHOCOLATE CHIP COOKIES 42
CRANBERRY DROP COOKIES 43
DATE DROP COOKIES 44
APPLESAUCE COOKIES 45
SPECIAL K FRUIT COOKIES 46
BANANA COOKIES 47
RAISIN COOKIES 48

NO-BAKE COOKIES 50

COCONUT DROP COOKIES 50
MOSAIC COOKIES 51
COCOA BALLS 52
QUICK CHOCOLATE COOKIES 53
OATMEAL NO BAKE COOKIES 54
RUM BALLS 55
CHOCOLATE FUDGE COOKIES 56
SKILLET COOKIES 57
APRICOT SNOWBALLS 58
CHOCOLATE CREAM COOKIES 59
ALMOND BARK COOKIES 60
WALNUT BALLS 61
CHOCOLATE OATMEAL COOKIES 62
CRUNCHY CHOCOLATE COOKIE 63
TINY PEANUT BUTTER BALLS 64

NUT COOKIES 66

CASHEW COOKIES 66
SALTED PEANUT COOKIES 67
SUNFLOWER NUT COOKIES 68
PECAN COOKIES 69
NUT DELIGHTS 70

BUTTER BALLS   71
CRUNCHY PEANUT COOKIES   72
MILLION DOLLAR COOKIES   73
MELT-A-WAY COOKIES   74
BLACK WALNUT COOKIES   75

PEANUT BUTTER COOKIES   77

WORLD'S EASIEST COOKIES   77
PEANUT BUTTER CHIP COOKIES   78
SNICKERS COOKIES   79
PEANUT BLOSSOMS   80
PEANUT BUTTER OATMEAL COOKIES   81
PEANUT BUTTER COOKIES   82
REESE PEANUT BUTTER SQUARES   83
CHOCOLATE PEANUT BUTTER BALLS   84

REFRIGERATOR COOKIES   86

OVERNIGHT COOKIES   86
WHIRLIGIG COOKIES   87
OATMEAL REFRIGERATOR COOKIES   88
BUTTERSCOTCH REFRIGERATOR COOKIES   89

SUGAR COOKIES   91

COUNTRY SUGAR COOKIES   91
CRISP SUGAR DROP COOKIES   92
SOUTHERN SUGAR COOKIES   93
KRISPIES SUGAR COOKIES   94
MELT-IN-YOUR-MOUTH SUGAR COOKIES   95
FROSTED SUGAR COOKIES   96

UNUSUALLY ODD COOKIES   98

POTATO CHIP COOKIES   98
BREAKFAST BACON COOKIES   99

BLACK BEAN BROWNIES   100
PORK AND BEAN BARS   101
CHINESE NOODLE COOKIES   102
CHOCOLATE REINDEER DROPPINGS   103

CHRISTMAS COOKIES   105

NO EGG CHRISTMAS BALLS   105
HOLIDAY COOKIES   106
CHRISTMAS COOKIES   107
CHERRY DROPS   108
ROLL OUT COOKIES   109
FRUITCAKE COOKIES   110
MOLASSES KRINKLES   111
CHOCOLATE-FRUIT CHRISTMAS COOKIES   112

COOKIE FROSTINGS   114

NEVER FAIL CARAMEL FROSTING   114
FUDGE FROSTING   115
BUTTER CREAM FROSTING   116
GERMAN COCONUT PECAN FROSTING   117
CREAM CHEESE FROSTING   118
EASY PENUCHE FROSTING   119

GINGER COOKIES   121

GINGERSNAPS   121
REFRIGERATOR GINGER COOKIES   122
BUTTERSCOTCH GINGERBREAD COOKIES   124
GINGERBREAD FILLING   125
COUNTRY RAISIN GINGERSNAPS   126

MISCELLANEOUS COOKIES   128

RICE KRISPIES COOKIES   128
BEST CHOCOLATE COOKIES   129

Coconut Cookies 130
Melting Moments 131
Low Cholesterol Cookies 132
Macaroons 133
Nutty Coconut Cookies 134
Coconut Drops 135
Pumpkin Cookies 136
Grandma's Swedish Cookies 137
M&M Cookies 138
Brown-Eyed Susans 139
Cream Cheese Cookies 140
Caramel Filled Snicker Doodles 141

BROWNIES 143

Coffee Blend Brownies 143
Easy No Bake Brownies 144
Brownie Cookies 145
Chewy Light Brownies 146
Cheesecake Mint Brownies 147
Best Brownies 148
Graham Cracker Brownies 149
Marshmallow Brownies 150
Chocolate Cherry Brownies 151
Frosted Brownies 152
Muffin Brownies 154
Coconut Brownies 155
Chocolate Date Brownies 156
Double Chocolate Brownies 157

BAR COOKIES 159

Yummy Layer Bars 159
No-Bake Peanut Butter Bars 160
Carrot Bars 161
Date Bars 162
Lemon Squares 163
Nut Goodie Bars 164

Too Easy Orange Bars   165
No Bake Chocolate Crunch Bars   166
Chewiest Granola Bars   167
Ten Dollar Bars   168
Caramel Cake Bars   169
Nut Variety Bars   170
Chocolate Oatmeal Bars   171
Toffee Bars   172
Butterscotch Squares   173
Honey of a Bar   174
Chocolate Glazed Bar Cookies   175
Baby Nathan Bars   176
Corn Flake Peanut Bars   177
Peach Bars   178
Fruit Cocktail Bars   179
Blueberry Bars   180
Apple Squares   181
Chocolate Chip Bars   182

Cookie Indulgence: 150 Easy Cookie Recipes

Warm from the oven and just waiting to accompany a glass of cold milk or a cup of steaming cocoa, nothing smells better than the aroma of freshly baked cookies. With Cookie Indulgence, you'll never run short of inspiration for quick and delicious cookies, bars and frostings to welcome friends and family home or to give as tasty gifts.

Browse through the pages of Cookie Indulgence to find just the right treat. With 150 favorites from Chocolate Chip or Oatmeal cookies to No-bake, Refrigerator and Christmas cookies, there is sure to be a recipe that will please even the most rigorous taste test your family can muster.

If your cookies need a little something extra, there are frosting recipes that will find you leaving a little extra in the bowl for personal taste testing. If you're looking for something unique, make sure to check out the Extremely Odd cookie section for recipes with ingredients you won't find on the average baking supply shelf.

So, sit back and relax with a good cookie while you scan the recipes and tips. Your next cookie baking session is sure to please everyone with goodies for gift giving, church bake sales or snacks for your family.

Use the Best Quality, Appropriate Ingredients

It bears repeating that you will have superior tasting cookies with the best texture if you use fresh, high quality ingredients.

Cheap chocolate or carob will give an off-flavor to the dough.

Use real vanilla extract. The flavor is far superior and a little goes a long way, so it's worth the price.

Using baking soda or baking powder past its expiration date jeopardizes the proper rising necessary to make a light cookie with the correct texture.

When possible, always use real butter for cookies. Replacing butter with margarine, which contains water, can change the texture and taste of your cookie. Also melt the butter and let cool to room temperature, rather than using softened butter. Melted butter will dissolve the sugar better in the creaming stage of the recipe.

How You Combine Your Ingredients Makes a Difference

Don't just dump all the ingredients in the bowl at once. If the recipe specifies creaming the egg and butter together, do so. This emulsifies the moist ingredients for ease in adding the dry ones. This also reduces mixing time and minimizes the possibility of tough dough.

Measure your ingredients precisely. Too little moisture results in dry cookies. Use too much moisture and you will end up with a flat layer of baked batter instead of a light and moist cookie.

Add dry ingredients like baking powder, baking soda, salt and spices to your flour, and mix them before adding the flour to the liquid. This ensures that the small amounts are well distributed throughout the dough.

Do not over-mix your dough after you add the dry ingredients. Over-mixing leads to tough dough or cookies that don't rise properly.

If the instructions state to chill before baking, refrigerate your dough. This refrigeration solidifies the butter, which helps reduce overspreading when the cookies are baked.

Use the Proper Equipment for Better Cookies

Just as your grandmother, and her grandmother before her, you can beat dough by hand. However, beating a batter or dough can be more than just mixing the ingredients. Beating also incorporates air into the mixture, which gives it a finer and a lighter texture. If the recipe calls for one, use an electric mixer. Your biceps will thank you, and your family will appreciate the light, tender texture of your tasty treats.

If you use a glass pan or a dark metal pan to bake bars, reduce the heat 25 degrees. Glass and dark metal hold the heat longer than light-colored metal pans.

You will get better baking results if you use a cookie sheet instead of a jelly roll pan. The lip of the jelly roll pan deflects some of the oven's heat. The use of a cookie sheet allows for increased air circulation and even baking.

If your oven doesn't bake your cookies evenly, rotate the cookie sheets from front to back and top to bottom midway through the cooking process.

Cookie Baking Accessories and Tools

Ditch the waxed-paper-on-the-counter routine your mother may have used to cool her cookies. Invest in some cooling racks. They're inexpensive and can be used for lots of other things besides cooling cookies.

If you have kids or grandkids, you need some cookie cutters. There are hundreds from which to choose. Baking and decorating cookies turns a rainy afternoon into a fun and creative activity time you can share with your little ones.

A nice set of cookie sheets is another good investment. There's a debate between the stoneware and the air-bake pan factions that's too hot to handle. However, both are made specifically for baking cookies, so you probably won't go wrong with either choice.

Parchment paper is necessary or helpful for some cookie recipes that burn easily or are sticky. Put a roll in your supply cupboard. You'll be glad you did.

A cookie press is a great way to make decorative cookies quickly. Assorted tips allow you to create different shapes for fun and festive cookies that look as good as those purchased from a bakery.

Bakery Style Cookies

What makes a bakery style cookie? Aside from quality ingredients and a good recipe, the main feature is the appearance. If you follow a few basic guidelines, any recipe and ingredients you use will make up into bakery style cookies.

Make your cookies uniform. If you're not good at estimating the size of the ball of dough, use a small scoop or spoon to measure the dough into equal quantities. This also ensures that the cookies will all bake consistently.

Bakery cookies are generally substantial in size. Use a sizeable scoop to make large, generous servings.

Ingredients such as nuts and chocolate are often large and chunky. Don't over-chop the nuts and use extra-large chips, or cut chocolate into ample bites.

Add sprinkles or sparkling colored sugar to cookies before baking.

If you're frosting your cookies, use concentrated icing color. This product is far more intense than regular food coloring and can be purchased at any craft store that sells cake-decorating supplies or at kitchen supply stores.

If you're baking bars, make the size uniform. Line the pan with parchment paper or aluminum foil, overlapping two inches over the edges. This step ensures you can easily remove the bars from the pan. After baking, do not cut the bars in the pan. Allow the pan to cool and use the parchment paper to lift and remove the contents. Now, you can cut the bars uniformly and separate them without ruining their shape. If your recipe calls for frosting, ice them after they are cut, so you have neat edges with no crumbs.

The Best Cookie Gifts from Your Kitchen

The best cookies are the ones that are made with love. Of course, there may be more to it than just that, but a pinch of love only adds to the sweetness of your gift.

Cookies that will be shipped should not be brittle or fragile. Choose chewy recipes that can be well packed. Another caution for shipping is heat. If you are sending cookies in warm weather, frosting them may not be a good idea. Iced cookies left sitting on loading docks or in trucks in the hot sun can quickly melt into a gloppy mess. Separate layers of cookies with wax paper or foil for extra protection.

Gifts of cookies and bars that go home with guests may not survive for long. However, make sure that the gift is fresh and the recipient knows whether the treat should remain at room temperature, be refrigerated or if it should be eaten within a certain time limit.

If you are giving any gift of food, make sure that the recipient is not allergic to any of the ingredients in your recipe. When in doubt, ask if there is anything they should not ingest.

If you have ethnic cookie recipes from your family or from those of friends, a package of cookies like grandma used to make will be an appreciated gift. Too frequently, recipes from our cultural heritage are lost or forgotten. A gift of Norwegian Krumkake or Hungarian Kifli will surely bring a smile of joy, as memories are mixed with crumbs from your delicious treat.

There are many hints and tips for baking cookies. I've included some common sense tips and advice that will help a beginner or an experienced cook make the most of baking and give the best results. These hints aren't complex or expensive, but they are basic preparation and cooking information that will produce flavorful and attractive baked goods.

Chocolate Chip Cookies

Double Chocolate Walnut Drops

1 1/2 cups flour
1 teaspoon baking powder
1/4 teaspoon salt
3/4 cup butter
3/4 cup white sugar
1 square unsweetened chocolate
1 egg
2 teaspoons milk
1 teaspoon vanilla
1/2 cup chocolate chips
3/4 cup nuts chopped

Melt the chocolate square and mix all ingredients together.
Bake at 350 degrees F for 10 to 12 minutes.

Chocolate Pudding Cookies

2 1/4 cups flour
1 teaspoon baking soda
3/4 cup packed brown sugar
1/4 cup sugar
1 cup butter, melted
1 package instant Jell-O® vanilla pudding, 4 serving size
2 eggs
1 teaspoon vanilla
2 cups chocolate chips
1 cup chopped nuts

Preheat oven to 375 degrees F. Combine butter, vanilla, sugars and pudding mix and beat until smooth and creamy. Mix in eggs. Mix and add flour and baking soda, then stir in nuts and chips. Drop by spoonfuls onto greased baking sheet. Bake for about 10 minutes.

Yield: 7 dozen

Cookie Brittle

1 cup butter
1 1/2 teaspoons vanilla
1 teaspoon salt
1 cup sugar
2 cups flour
1/2 cup nuts
1 cup chocolate chips

Mix all the ingredients and press evenly into ungreased 15x10 inch pan. Bake at 375 degrees F for 25 minutes. Cool and then break into irregular shapes.

Excellent Chocolate Chip Cookies

1 cup sugar
1 cup brown sugar, packed
1 cup butter, melted
2 teaspoons vanilla
2 eggs
1 teaspoon baking soda
3 cups flour
1/2 teaspoon salt
1/2 teaspoons cream of tartar
2 cups semi-sweet chocolate chips

Mix the brown and white sugar and butter together. Add the eggs and vanilla. In a separate dish, put 2 teaspoons of hot water and add the baking soda. When the baking soda is dissolved, add it to the cookie batter. Add the flour, cream of tartar, salt and chocolate chips. Bake at 350 degrees F on ungreased cookie sheet for 10 to 12 minutes.

All-In-One Cookie

1 cup butter, melted
2 teaspoons vanilla
1/2 teaspoon salt
1 cup sugar
3/4 cup brown sugar
2 eggs
1 teaspoon baking soda
2 1/2 cups flour
1 10-ounce bag white chocolate chips

Preheat oven to 375 degrees F. In a bowl, cream both sugars, butter, vanilla and salt. Mix until creamy. Add eggs and beat well. Stir together flour and baking soda; gradually add to butter mixture and mix well. Stir in the white chips. Drop by spoonfuls on ungreased sheet. Bake 8 to 10 minutes.

Yield: 5 dozen

Chocolate Krinkle Cookies

1 cup chocolate chips
1 cup brown sugar, packed
1/3 cup vegetable oil
2 eggs
1 teaspoon vanilla
1 cup flour
1/4 teaspoon salt
1 teaspoon baking powder
1/2 cup chopped walnuts
1/2 cup powdered sugar for dipping

Melt chocolate chips and combine with the oil and sugar. Add eggs and beat well. Add vanilla. Mix flour, salt and baking powder and add to the chocolate mixture. Stir in walnuts. Chill dough. When dough is chilled, roll spoonfuls of dough in powdered sugar. Place on greased cookie sheet. Bake at 350 degrees F for 10 to 12 minutes.

Yield: 4 dozen

Honey Chocolate Chip Cookies

1/2 cup honey
1/2 cup butter
1 egg
1/2 teaspoon vanilla
1 1/2 cups flour
1/2 teaspoon salt
1/2 teaspoon baking soda
1/4 teaspoon baking powder
1/2 cup nuts
1 cup chocolate chips

Cream honey and butter together. Add egg and vanilla and mix well. Add dry ingredients. Add nuts and chips and stir well. Drop by spoonfuls on ungreased cookie sheet. Bake at 350 degrees F for 10 to 12 minutes.

Pumpkin Chip Cookies

1/2 cup butter, melted
1 1/2 cups sugar
1 teaspoon vanilla
1 egg
1 cup canned pumpkin
2 1/2 cups flour
1/2 teaspoon salt
1 teaspoon nutmeg
1 teaspoon baking powder
1 teaspoon cinnamon
1 teaspoon baking soda
1 cup chocolate chips
1/2 cup nuts

Cream butter and sugar. Add egg and vanilla and mix well. Add pumpkin. Add dry ingredients. Add nuts and chips and stir well. Drop by teaspoon on cookie sheet. Bake 350 degrees F 15 minutes.

Dolittle Cookies

2 cups flour
1/2 teaspoon salt
1 teaspoon baking soda
1/2 teaspoon baking powder
1 cup white sugar
1 cup brown sugar
1 cup butter
2 eggs
2 cups rolled oats
2 cups chocolate chips
1 teaspoon vanilla

Mix together flour, salt, baking soda and baking powder. In another bowl, blend the white sugar, brown sugar, butter and eggs. Add flour mixture and mix well. Add the oats, chocolate chips and vanilla. Drop by spoonfuls on ungreased cookie sheet. Bake for 15 minutes in a 350 degrees F oven.

Bakery Chocolate Chip Cookies

1 1/2 cups flour
1/2 teaspoon salt
1/4 teaspoon cinnamon
1/2 teaspoon baking soda
3/4 cup brown sugar, packed
1/3 cup white sugar
1 1/2 cups semi-sweet chocolate chips or chocolate chunks
2 1/4 teaspoons vanilla extract
1 egg
1 egg yolk
1/2 cup butter, melted

Preheat the oven to 325 degrees F. Mix together the white and brown sugar in a large bowl. Add the melted butter to the sugars and mix well. Add the egg, egg yolk and vanilla and mix well until light and creamy. Mix the flour, salt, cinnamon and baking soda together and add to egg mixture. Add the chocolate chips.

Grease a cookie sheet or use parchment paper. Drop the dough by large spoonfuls (bakery style) on a cookie sheet and flatten cookies a bit. Bake the cookies for 15 to 16 minutes or until edges are turning light brown.

Deluxe Chocolate Chip Cookies

2 1/4 cups flour
1 teaspoon salt
1 teaspoon baking soda
3/4 cup brown sugar
3/4 cup granulated sugar
1 cup butter, melted
2 large eggs
2 cups semi-sweet chocolate chips
1 teaspoon vanilla
1/2 cup shredded coconut
1/2 cup heath toffee bits
1/2 cup chopped pecans

Mix flour, salt and baking soda; set aside. Cream the butter and sugars together. Add eggs to sugar mixture; mix well after adding each. Add vanilla. Add flour mixture gradually. Stir in chocolate chips, coconut, toffee bits and pecans. Drop by heaping spoonfuls on ungreased cookie sheet. Bake at 375 degrees F for 10 to 12 minutes.

Zucchini Chocolate Chip Cookies

3/4 cup butter
1 1/2 cups sugar
1 egg
1 teaspoon vanilla
1 1/2 cups zucchini, peeled and grated
2 1/2 cups flour
2 teaspoons baking powder
1 teaspoon cinnamon
1/2 teaspoon salt
1 cup almonds, coarsely chopped
1 cup semi-sweet chocolate chips

Preheat oven to 350 degrees F. Cream the butter and sugar; add the egg and vanilla. Stir in the zucchini. Mix in flour, baking powder, salt and cinnamon. Add the almonds and chocolate chips. Drop by heaping teaspoons onto a greased cookie sheet. Bake for 15 minutes or until lightly browned. Sprinkle with powdered sugar if desired.

Oatmeal Cookies

Oatmeal Cookies

Apple Oatmeal Cookies

1 cup butter, melted
1 cup brown sugar, packed
1 teaspoon vanilla
2 eggs
2 cups flour
1 teaspoon cinnamon
1/2 teaspoon salt
2 teaspoons baking powder
1/2 cup milk
2 cups quick-cooking oats
1/2 teaspoon cloves
Apple jelly

Beat together butter and brown sugar until light and fluffy. Beat in eggs and vanilla until blended. In another bowl, mix together flour, baking powder, cinnamon, cloves and salt. Alternately beat the flour mixture into cream mixture with milk. Stir in oats. Set aside 3/4 cup of dough for making top of cookies.

Drop dough by slightly rounded spoonfuls onto lightly greased cookie sheets. Make depression in center of each cookie. Fill each with slightly rounded 1/2 teaspoon apple jelly. Top with a dab of cookie dough. Bake at 350 degrees F for 8 to 12 minutes. Yield: 6 dozen

Coffee Shop Oatmeal Cookies

1 cup brown sugar
1/2 cup white sugar
1 cup butter
2 eggs
1/4 cup milk or buttermilk
1 teaspoon vanilla
2 cups quick oats
2 cups flour
1/2 teaspoon cinnamon
1/2 teaspoon salt
1 teaspoon baking soda
2 teaspoons baking powder
1 cup raisins
1 cup chocolate chips
1 cup nuts (optional)

Cream sugars and butter. Add eggs one at a time, beating after each addition. Stir in milk, vanilla and oats. Add dry ingredients. Mix thoroughly. Add raisins, chips and nuts. Drop by spoonfuls onto greased cookie sheet and bake at 350 degrees F for 10 to 12 minutes or until golden brown

Yield: 60 cookies

Pioneer Cornflake Cookies

1 cup white sugar
1 cup brown sugar
1 cup butter
1 cup Crisco® oil
1 egg
Pinch of salt
1/2 teaspoon almond flavoring
1/2 teaspoon vanilla
1/2 cup nuts
1 teaspoon baking soda in 1 teaspoon milk
1 teaspoon cream of tartar
3 1/2 cups flour
1 cup quick oats
1 cup cornflakes
1 cup coconut

Mix in the order listed. Drop by spoonfuls on cookie sheet. Press flat with bottom of glass dipped in sugar. Bake 10 minutes at 350 degrees F or until lightly browned.

Cracker Jack Cookies

1 cup white sugar
1 cup brown sugar
1 cup butter
2 eggs
2 teaspoons vanilla
1 1/2 cups flour
1 teaspoon baking powder
1 teaspoon baking soda
1 cup coconut
2 cups quick oats
2 cups Rice Krispies® cereal
1 cup semi-sweet chocolate chips

Preheat oven to 350 degrees F. Cream together sugars and butter. Add eggs and vanilla; mix well. Mix flour, baking soda, and baking powder and beat into creamed mixture. Add coconut, oats, Rice Krispies and chocolate chips, in that order. Drop onto cookie sheet and bake for 10 to 12 minutes.

Oatmeal Gem Cookies

2 cups butter
2 cups granulated sugar
2 cups brown sugar
2 teaspoons vanilla
4 eggs
2 teaspoons salt
1 teaspoon baking soda
3 cups flour
6 cup quick oats
2 cups semi-sweet chocolate chips

Preheat oven to 350 degrees F. Cream together butter and sugars. Add vanilla and eggs mixing well after each egg. Add salt, baking soda, and flour; mix well. Blend in oats and then add the chocolate chips. Drop by spoonfuls onto an ungreased cookie sheet. Bake for about 10 minutes or until golden brown.

Moist Oatmeal Cookies

1 cup butter
1 cup white sugar
2 eggs
1/2 cup hot raisin juice
1 teaspoon baking soda
2 cups regular oats
2 cups flour
1 teaspoon cinnamon
1 teaspoon nutmeg
1 teaspoon vanilla
1 1/2 cups boiled raisins
1 teaspoon salt
1/2 cup nuts

Boil raisins for 10 minutes. Save 1/2 cup raisin juice. Let the raisins cool a bit, then mix in order listed. Bake at 350 degrees F for 10 to 12 minutes.

Double Chocolate Oatmeal Cookies

1 cup sugar
1 cup melted butter
1 egg
1/4 cup water
1 teaspoon vanilla
1 1/4 cups enriched flour
1/3 cup cocoa
1/2 teaspoon baking soda
3 cups quick-cooking oats
1 cup chocolate chips

Preheat oven to 350 degrees F. Mix sugar, melted butter, egg, water and vanilla. Stir in remaining ingredients. Drop dough by rounded spoonfuls on an ungreased cookie sheet. Bake until almost no dent remains when touched, 10 to 12 minutes.

Yield: 5 1/2 dozen

Oatmeal Raisin Cookies

1 cup butter, melted
1 cup brown sugar, packed
1 teaspoon vanilla
2 eggs
1 1/2 cups flour
1 teaspoon baking soda
1 teaspoon cinnamon
1/2 teaspoon salt
3 cups quick oats
1 cup raisins

Preheat oven to 350 degrees F. Cream together the butter and sugar until creamy. Add vanilla and eggs and mix well. Add flour, baking soda, salt and cinnamon. Stir in oats and raisins. Drop by spoonfuls on ungreased cookie sheets. Bake 10 to 12 minutes or until golden brown.

Yield: 4 dozen

Chocolate Chip Oatmeal Cookies

2 cups flour
2 teaspoons baking powder
1/2 teaspoon salt
2 cups rolled oats
1 cup brown sugar
1 cup butter
1/3 cup milk
2 eggs
3/4 cup chopped walnuts
1 cup chocolate chips

Thoroughly blend together all dry ingredients, except chocolate chips and nuts. Add all liquids and mix. Dough will be stiff. Add chocolate chips and nuts and mix by hand. Drop on greased cookie sheet. Bake at 350 degrees F for 15 minutes.

Yield: 3 dozen

Cherry Oatmeal Cookies

1 1/4 cups flour
1 teaspoon baking powder
1/2 teaspoon baking soda
3/4 teaspoon salt
3/4 cup butter
1/2 cup white sugar
1 1/2 cups brown sugar, packed
2 unbeaten eggs
1 teaspoon vanilla
2 1/2 cups quick oats
1 cup nuts
1 cup raisins, plump in water

Mix together the flour, baking powder, baking soda and salt. Cream butter and sugars together; add eggs and vanilla. Blend in dry ingredients. Add oats, nuts and raisins. Drop by spoonfuls onto lightly greased baking sheets. Bake at 350 degrees F for 10 minutes.

Skinny Oatmeal Cookies

1 cup butter
1/2 cup brown sugar
1/2 cup white sugar
1/2 teaspoon salt
1/2 teaspoon baking soda
1/4 cup hot water
1 teaspoon vanilla
3 cups quick oats
1 cup flour

Cream butter, brown sugar, white sugar and salt well. Dissolve baking soda in hot water and add to creamed mixture. Add vanilla, oats and flour. Mix well. There are no eggs! Drop by teaspoonful on greased cookie sheet. With fork dipped in hot water, flatten and shape cookie to very thin. Bake at 350 degrees F for 8 to 10 minutes.

Yield: 76 cookies

Fruit Cookies

Banana Chocolate Chip Cookies

2 1/2 cups flour
2 teaspoons baking powder
1/2 teaspoon salt
1/4 teaspoon baking soda
2/3 cup butter, melted
1 cup white sugar
1 teaspoon vanilla
2 eggs
1 cup bananas, mashed
2 cups semi-sweet chocolate chips

Preheat oven to 400 degrees F. Mix the flour, salt, baking powder and baking soda together and set aside.

Cream the butter and sugar until fluffy and light. Beat in the vanilla and eggs. Mix in the bananas. Add the flour mixture and mix. Stir in the chocolate chips. Drop by spoonfuls onto greased cookie sheets. Bake for 12 to 15 minutes.

Cranberry Drop Cookies

1/2 cup butter
1 cup sugar
1 cup brown sugar
1 egg
1/4 cup milk
2 teaspoons lemon juice
3 cups flour
1 teaspoon baking powder
1/2 teaspoon baking soda
1 cup dried cranberries
1 cup nuts, chopped

Cream butter and sugars; add egg, milk and lemon juice. Add flour, baking powder and baking soda. Mix well and stir in cranberries and nuts. Bake at 375 degrees F for 13 to 15 minutes or until golden brown.

Yield: 5 dozen

Date Drop Cookies

1/2 cup butter
1 1/2 cups brown sugar
1 teaspoon vanilla
2 eggs
2 1/2 cups flour
1 teaspoon baking soda
1/2 teaspoon salt
1/2 teaspoon baking powder
1 cup sour cream
1 cup chopped nuts
4 dozen dates, cut up

Cream butter and sugar; add eggs and vanilla and mix well. Add flour, baking soda, salt and baking powder and mix. Add sour cream, nuts and dates. Drop by spoonfuls on cookie sheet. Bake in 375 degrees F oven for 10 to 12 minutes. Do not overbake. When cool, frost with powdered sugar frosting.

Yield: 4 dozen

Applesauce Cookies

3/4 cup butter
1 cup brown sugar
1 egg
1/2 cup applesauce
1 cup raisins
2 1/4 cups flour
1 teaspoon baking soda
Pinch of salt
3/4 teaspoon cinnamon
1/4 teaspoon cloves
1/2 cup nuts (optional)

Mix butter, egg, and sugar. Stir in applesauce. Add dry ingredients. Stir in chopped raisins (boiled a little) and nuts. Drop by teaspoon on cookie sheet. Bake at 375 degrees F for 10 to 12 minutes.

Special K Fruit Cookies

1 cup flour
1/2 teaspoon baking powder
1 1/4 teaspoon salt
1/4 teaspoon baking soda
1/2 cup butter, melted
1 cup brown sugar
1 egg
1/2 teaspoon vanilla
1 cup flaked coconut
1 cup raisins
2 cups Special K® cereal

Preheat oven to 350 degrees F. Mix together flour, baking powder, salt and baking soda. Set aside. Mix melted butter with brown sugar, then egg and vanilla, mix well. Add dry ingredients.

Add coconut, raisins, and 1 cup of the Special K®. Crush the remaining cup of Special K and roll balls of dough in it. Bake on ungreased cookie sheet for about 10 to 12 minutes.

Banana Cookies

1/2 cup brown sugar
1/2 cup white sugar
3/4 cup butter
1 teaspoon salt
1 egg, beaten
1 cup bananas (2 or 3)
1/4 teaspoon nutmeg
3/4 teaspoon cinnamon
1/2 teaspoon baking soda
1/2 cup coconut
1/2 cup dates or raisins
1/2 cup nuts
1 3/4 cups quick oats
1 1/2 cups flour

Mix together all ingredients. Drop by spoonfuls onto cookie sheet. Bake at 350 degrees F for 12 to 15 minutes.

Raisin Cookies

1 lb. raisins
1/2 cup butter
1 1/4 cups brown sugar
2 eggs
1 teaspoon salt
1 teaspoon cinnamon
1 teaspoon nutmeg
1 teaspoon cloves
1 teaspoon baking soda
3 cups flour
1 teaspoon vanilla
1/2 cup raisin water
1 cup nuts (optional)

Cover the raisins with water and simmer for 10 minutes. Drain raisins, saving 1/2 cup of liquid, and let cool. Cream butter and sugar together. Add eggs and mix well. Mix the dry ingredients, add to mixture along with the raisin water. Add vanilla and nuts; mix. Drop by spoonfuls on greased baking sheet. Bake for 15 minutes at 350 degrees F.

Yield: 3 1/2 dozen

No-Bake Cookies

Coconut Drop Cookies

2 teaspoons butter, melted
3 teaspoons water
1 teaspoon vanilla
2 cups powdered sugar
1/2 cup powdered milk
3 cups coconut
Mint chocolate chips (10 ounce package)

Mix butter, water and vanilla. Add powdered sugar and milk. Mix well. Add coconut.

Drop and roll into small balls. Place on waxed paper. Let stand about 10 minutes. Melt 1 package mint chocolate chips in microwave and drop 1/2 teaspoon on each cookie. Optional - Sprinkle a few sugar candies on the top before chocolate hardens.

Mosaic Cookies

1/2 large bar baking chocolate
2 teaspoons butter
1 cup powdered sugar
1 egg
3/4 cup walnuts
1 package colored tiny marshmallows
Graham cracker crumbs

Melt butter and chocolate in microwave. Beat egg, add powdered sugar; add to chocolate mixture. Add nuts and marshmallows to the mixture. Roll in graham cracker crumbs. Roll in 4 foil rolls (butter hands). Freeze until serving time. Slice.

Cocoa Balls

1/2 cup butter
2 cups brown sugar
3 teaspoons cocoa
1 grated apple

Mix all the above ingredients. Boil for one minute.

Add:

3 cups quick oats
1 cup nuts
1 teaspoon vanilla

Roll dough to make balls and then roll in coconut.

Quick Chocolate Cookies

2 cups white sugar
3 teaspoons cocoa
1/2 cup butter
1/2 cup milk
1/4 teaspoon salt
Vanilla
3 cups quick oats
1/2 cup coconut
1/2 cup nuts

Mix the sugar, cocoa, butter, salt, vanilla and milk in a pan and boil for 1 minute. Stir in oats, coconut and nuts. Remove from stove and drop by spoonfuls on wax paper.

Oatmeal No Bake Cookies

1/2 cup evaporated milk
1/2 cup cocoa
1/2 cup butter
2 cups sugar
1 teaspoon vanilla
3 cups quick oats
1/2 cup peanut butter

Mix butter, milk, cocoa and sugar in a pan. Bring this mixture to a boil and cook for one minute. Remove from heat and add vanilla, oats and peanut butter. Stir mixture well until peanut butter is mixed. Drop on wax paper.

Yield: 3 dozen

Rum Balls

1 cup vanilla wafer crumbs
1 cup powdered sugar
2 tablespoons unsweetened cocoa
1 cup ground almonds
1/4 cup golden rum (or more if desired)

Mix ingredients together until well blended. Mold mixture into small balls. Then coat each ball with equal amounts of additional cocoa and powdered sugar.

Yield: 3 dozen

Chocolate Fudge Cookies

1/2 cup milk
1/2 cup butter
4 tablespoons cocoa
2 cups sugar
1 to 2 teaspoons vanilla
2 1/2 cups quick oats
1 cup chopped nuts

Boil milk, butter, cocoa and sugar for 1 1/2 minutes. Remove from heat; add vanilla, oatmeal and nuts. Beat until blended; then drop on wax paper by teaspoons. Coconut or dates may be added, if desired.

Skillet Cookies

1/2 cup butter
3/4 cup sugar
1 cup dates, cut fine
1 tablespoon milk
1 egg, beaten
1/2 teaspoon salt
3 cups Rice Krispies®
1 cup coconut

Melt butter, add sugar and dates. Cook together over low heat to boiling point. Remove from heat, add egg, milk and salt. Return to heat and boil 2 minutes stirring constantly. Cool slightly and add to Rice Krispies®. Mix well and cool enough to handle. Roll into balls and roll in coconut.

Apricot Snowballs

1 1/2 cups dried apricots
2 cups coconut (ground)
2/3 cups sweetened condensed milk
Powdered sugar

Mix the first three ingredients well. Roll into small balls; then roll in powdered sugar. Chill.

Chocolate Cream Cookies

3 cups oats
1 cup coconut
4 teaspoons cocoa
1/2 cup milk
1/2 cup butter
2 cups sugar
1 teaspoon vanilla
1/2 cup chopped nuts

Mix oats, coconut, and cocoa in large bowl; set aside. Heat milk, butter, and sugar in saucepan; bring to a boil. Add wet ingredients to dry; mix well. Add vanilla and nuts. Drop by spoonfuls onto wax paper.

Almond Bark Cookies

1/2 large package almond bark
2 cups broken stick pretzels
2 cups Rice Krispies®
1 or 2 cups dry roasted peanuts

Melt almond bark in microwave. Add the pretzels, Rice
Krispies® and peanuts and mix well. Drop on wax paper to
cool.

Walnut Balls

2 cups vanilla wafer crumbs
1/3 cup granulated sugar
1/8 teaspoon salt
1/2 teaspoon cinnamon
1/2 cup maraschino cherries, chopped
1 cup walnuts, cut in half
1 teaspoon lemon juice
2/3 cup sweetened condensed milk

Mix together vanilla wafers, sugar, salt, cinnamon, cherries and walnuts. Add lemon juice and sweetened condensed milk and mix well. Form into 1" balls. Roll in sugar and trim with nut halves.

Yield: 4 dozen

Chocolate Oatmeal Cookies

2 cups sugar
1/2 cup milk
1/3 cup cocoa
1/4 cup butter
3 cups quick oats
1/2 cup peanut butter
1/2 cup coconut
1 teaspoon vanilla

Combine sugar, milk, cocoa and butter. Boil for 1 minute. Remove from heat. Mix in quick oats, peanut butter, coconut and vanilla. Drop by spoonfuls on wax paper or parchment paper.

Yield: 2 1/2 dozen

Crunchy Chocolate Cookie

2 cups sugar
1/2 cup butter
1/2 cup milk
1 teaspoon vanilla
3 cups quick oats
1/2 cup baking cocoa
1 cup coconut
1 cup chopped walnuts

Boil first 3 ingredients together for 1 minute. Quickly add remaining ingredients. Mix and drop by spoonfuls on waxed paper.

Nut Cookies

Cashew Cookies

1/2 cup butter
1 cup brown sugar, packed
1/4 teaspoon salt
2 cups flour
1 egg
3/4 teaspoon baking soda
3/4 teaspoon baking powder
1/2 cup sour cream
1/2 teaspoon vanilla
1 3/4 cups salted cashews chopped

Mix all ingredients and drop by teaspoon on greased cookie sheet. Bake 10 minutes at 375 degrees F.

Salted Peanut Cookies

1 1/2 cups flour
1 cup brown sugar
1 cup white sugar
2 eggs
1 teaspoon vanilla
1 cup butter
1 teaspoon baking soda
1 teaspoon baking powder
3 cups rolled oats
1 cup salted peanuts

Cream sugars, butter, eggs and vanilla together. Add flour, baking soda and baking powder. Add oats and peanuts. Drop by teaspoon on greased cookie sheet. Bake at 350 degrees F for 10 to 12 minutes.

Sunflower Nut Cookies

2 cups sugar
3 cups flour
1 teaspoon baking soda
1 teaspoon baking powder
1 cup butter
1 cup salted, roasted sunflower kernels
1 cup margarine or shortening
1 teaspoon vanilla
1 cup flaked coconut

Cream the butter, margarine and sugar together. Add the vanilla. Mix the dry ingredients together and add to the butter mixture. Add coconut and sunflower kernels. Shape into four, 2 inch rolls and refrigerate at least 2 hours. Slice and bake about 10 minutes at 375 degrees F.

Pecan Cookies

1 cup butter
4 teaspoons powdered sugar
1 teaspoon vanilla
1 teaspoon water
2 cups flour
Whole pecans

Mix all the ingredients together except pecans. Roll into balls. Roll each ball in powdered sugar. Place a pecan on top of each ball and bake at 375 degrees F for 15 minutes.

Nut Delights

1/2 cup butter
1 cup packed brown sugar
1 egg
1 teaspoon vanilla
1 3/4 cups flour
1 teaspoon salt
3/4 teaspoon baking soda
1/2 cup nuts

Cream sugar, butter, egg and vanilla together. Add flour, baking soda and salt. Mix in the nuts. Refrigerate for a few hours or overnight. Bake at 375 degrees for 8 to 10 minutes.

Butter Balls

3 tablespoons confectioner's sugar
1/2 cup butter
1 teaspoon vanilla
1 cup flour
1/2 cup chopped nuts
Extra confectioner's sugar (for dusting)

Mix ingredients together thoroughly except for extra sugar. Roll dough into 1" balls. Bake at 400 degrees F 12 to 15 minutes. Dust with confectioner's sugar while warm.

Crunchy Peanut Cookies

1/2 cup brown sugar
1/2 cup white sugar
3/4 cup butter
1 egg
1/2 teaspoon baking soda
1/2 teaspoon baking powder
1/2 teaspoon vanilla
1 1/4 cups flour
1 cup quick oats
1 cup corn flakes
1/2 cup coconut
1/2 cup salted peanuts

Cream butter and sugars together. Add egg, baking soda, baking powder and vanilla. Mix and add flour, oats, corn flakes, coconut and salted peanuts. Drop by spoonfuls on ungreased cookie sheet. Bake for 8 to 10 minutes at 350 degrees F.

Million Dollar Cookies

1 cup butter
1/2 cup brown sugar
1/2 cup white sugar
1 teaspoon vanilla
1 egg
2 cups flour
1/2 teaspoon salt
1/2 teaspoon baking soda
1/2 cup chopped nuts

Cream together the butter and sugars. Add egg, vanilla, flour, baking soda, salt and nuts. Mix and roll into small balls. Roll each ball in granulated sugar. Place on greased cookie sheet. Flatten each with the bottom of a small glass dipped in sugar. Bake at 350 degrees F for 10 minutes.

Melt-A-Way Cookies

1 cup sugar
1/2 cup butter
1 egg
1/2 cup oil
1 teaspoon vanilla
2 1/2 cups flour
1 teaspoon baking soda
1 teaspoon cream of tartar
1 cup finely chopped pecans

Cream together butter, sugar, egg, oil and vanilla. Add flour, baking soda, cream of tartar and pecans. Mix well. Roll into balls. Dip small rimmed glass in sugar and flatten cookies. Bake on ungreased cookie sheet at 350 degrees F for 10 to 12 minutes.

Black Walnut Cookies

2 cups brown sugar, packed
4 eggs, beaten
1/2 cup flour
1/2 teaspoon salt
1/2 teaspoon baking powder
4 cups black walnuts, chopped

Preheat oven to 375 degrees F. In a medium bowl, beat eggs and sugar together until well mixed. Mix together the flour, salt and baking powder, gradually add to the egg mixture. Stir in the nuts until they are evenly distributed. Drop by spoonfuls onto greased cookie sheet. Bake for 10 to 12 minutes.

Peanut Butter Cookies

World's Easiest Cookies

1 cup peanut butter
1 cup sugar
1 egg

Mix all 3 ingredients together. Drop by spoonfuls or shape into small balls on cookie sheet. Bake at 350 degrees F for 10 to 12 minutes.

Peanut Butter Chip Cookies

1 cup granulated sugar
1 cup brown sugar, packed
1/2 cup peanut butter
2 eggs
2 teaspoons vanilla
2 1/2 cups flour
1 teaspoon baking soda
1 teaspoon salt
2 cups milk chocolate chips

Beat sugars and peanut butter in a large bowl until light and fluffy. Blend in eggs and vanilla. Mix in flour, baking soda and salt. Stir in chocolate chips. Drop by rounded spoonfuls onto ungreased cookie sheet. Bake at 350 degrees F for 10 to 12 minutes.

Snickers Cookies

1 cup creamy peanut butter
1 cup butter
1 cup brown sugar
1 cup sugar
2 teaspoons vanilla
2 eggs
3 cups flour
1 teaspoon baking soda
1 teaspoon baking powder
60 miniature-sized Snickers® bars

Preheat oven to 350 degrees F. Cream peanut butter, butter, brown sugar and sugar together; add vanilla and eggs. Combine flour, baking soda, and baking powder and add to creamed mixture.

Use 1 tablespoon of dough and flatten into a circular shape. Place a Snickers in the center of the dough and fold dough over the candy. Roll the dough in your hands to form a smooth ball. Bake for 10 to 12 minutes.

Peanut Blossoms

1 1/3 cups flour
1 teaspoon baking soda
1/2 teaspoon salt
1/2 cup butter
1/3 cup peanut butter
1/2 cup sugar
1/2 cup brown sugar
1 beaten egg
1 teaspoon vanilla
18 chocolate candy kisses, unwrapped

Cream butter and peanut butter. Add sugars, egg, and vanilla. Blend in flour, baking soda, and salt. Shape in balls. Roll in sugar. Bake at 375 degrees F for 12 minutes on greased cookie sheet. Put chocolate kisses on each cookie after removing from oven.

Peanut Butter Oatmeal Cookies

1 cup butter
1 cup granulated sugar
1 cup brown sugar, packed
2 eggs
1 cup peanut butter
2 cups flour
1 cup quick oats
2 teaspoons baking soda
1/2 teaspoon salt

Cream butter and sugars together. Add eggs and peanut butter. Mix well. Stir in flour, oats, baking soda and salt. Shape into 1 1/4" balls. Place on ungreased cookie sheet. Flatten crisscross style with fork. Bake at 350 degrees F for 10 to 12 minutes.

Yield: 7 dozen

Peanut Butter Cookies

1/2 cup brown sugar
1/2 cup granulated sugar
1/2 cup peanut butter
1/2 cup butter
1 egg
1 1/4 cups flour
1/4 teaspoon salt
1/2 teaspoon baking soda

Cream sugars, peanut butter, butter and egg together. Add flour, salt and baking soda into peanut butter mixture. Shape dough into 1" balls, flatten with a fork and place on greased cookie sheet. Bake at 375 degrees F for 10 minutes until brown.

Reese Peanut Butter Squares

1 cup butter
1 1/2 cups crushed graham crackers
1 cup chunky peanut butter
2 1/2 cups confectioner's sugar
12 ounce chocolate Hershey's bar

Melt butter. Mix in graham cracker crumbs. Add peanut butter and sugar and mix together thoroughly. Press into greased 9x13 inch pan. Melt chocolate in microwave. Spread chocolate over top. Place in refrigerator until hard. Heat knife to cut into squares.

Chocolate Peanut Butter Balls

4 3/4 cups powdered sugar
1/2 cup butter
2 cups peanut butter
3 cups Rice Krispies®

Mix all ingredients above together. Form into little balls (gumball size). Place on cookie sheet. Chill. In double boiler or microwave, melt:

1 large Hershey bar
1 cup semi-sweet chocolate chips
1/2 bar paraffin wax

Dip balls in chocolate mixture (use tongs). Place on wax paper to set.

Refrigerator Cookies

Refrigerator Cookies

Overnight Cookies

1 cup butter
1 cup shortening or margarine
1 cup brown sugar
1 cup white sugar
3 eggs, beaten
1 teaspoon baking soda
2 teaspoons vanilla
3/4 cup walnuts, chopped
6 1/4 cups flour

Cream together butter, shortening and sugars. Add the eggs. Mix baking soda in a little water and add to mixture then add vanilla and chopped walnuts. Mix in flour. Form 3 rolls and let stand overnight in refrigerator. Slice and bake until light brown 375 degrees F for 10 to 12 minutes.

Whirligig Cookies

1/2 cup butter
1/2 cup brown sugar
1/2 cup sugar
1/2 cup cream peanut butter
1 egg
1 1/4 cups flour
1/2 teaspoon baking soda
1/2 teaspoon salt
1 cup chocolate chips

Cream butter, sugars and peanut butter. Add egg and mix. Combine the flour, salt and baking soda; add to the cream mixture. Roll the dough into an oblong shape, about 1/4 inch thick. (Hint: Roll dough between 2 floured sheets of wax paper.)

Melt chocolate chips in microwave. Spread chocolate on the dough. Roll up the dough jelly-roll fashion. Chill the dough logs for 20 minutes. Slice 1/4 inch thick pieces and place on cookie sheet. Bake at 375 degrees F for 6 to 7 minutes.

Oatmeal Refrigerator Cookies

1 1/2 cup flour
1 teaspoon baking soda
1 1/2 teaspoons salt
1 cup butter
1 cup white sugar
1 cup brown sugar, packed
2 eggs, beaten
1 teaspoon vanilla
3 cups quick oats

Mix flour, baking soda and salt. Cream butter and sugars and beat until light and fluffy. Beat in eggs and vanilla. Blend in dry ingredients; mix in oats. Shape into rolls 2 inches across, wrap in waxed paper. Chill thoroughly or overnight. Cut in thin slices. Bake or ungreased cookie sheet 400 degrees F for 8 minutes.

Yield: 6 dozen

Butterscotch Refrigerator Cookies

2 cups brown sugar
1 cup butter
2 eggs
3 1/2 cups flour
1 teaspoon cream of tartar
1 teaspoon baking soda
1/8 teaspoon salt
1 teaspoon vanilla
1 cup nuts, dates or coconut

Cream sugar and butter. Add eggs and beat until well mixed.
Add flour, cream of tartar, salt and baking soda. Mix well.
Add vanilla and nuts. Shape into desired loaf. Chill. Slice and
bake at 375 degrees F until browned.

Sugar Cookies

Sugar Cookies

Country Sugar Cookies

1/2 cup butter
1 cup sugar
1 egg
2 cups flour
1/2 teaspoon vanilla

Cream together butter and sugar. Blend in egg. Add flour. Blend vanilla into mixture. Bake at 375 degrees F for 10 to 12 minutes.

Optional - Glaze cookies with 3/4 cup powdered sugar mixed with 3 to 4 teaspoons water. Glaze and decorate cookies while still warm.

Krispies Sugar Cookies

1 cup butter
1 cup sugar
1 cup brown sugar
1 egg
1 cup cooking oil
1 teaspoon vanilla
1 teaspoon cream of tartar
1 teaspoon baking soda
1 teaspoon salt
3 1/2 cups flour
1 cup coconut
1 cup oats
1 cup nuts, optional
1 cup Rice Krispies®

Preheat oven to 350 degrees F. Cream together butter and sugars. Add egg and oil, mixing after each. Add vanilla. Mix together cream of tartar, baking soda, salt, and flour. Add to creamed mixture. Stir in coconut, oats, nuts, and Rice Krispies. Roll into balls and flatten with glass dipped in sugar. Bake for 10 to 15 minutes.

Optional: Melt chocolate chips in microwave. Drop about a teaspoon of chocolate on the bottom of one cookie, top with another cookie the same size.

Melt-In-Your-Mouth Sugar Cookies

1 cup mayonnaise (not salad dressing)
1 teaspoon vanilla
2 cups flour
1/4 teaspoon salt
1 teaspoon baking soda
1 cup white sugar

Mix mayonnaise and vanilla together. Combine flour, salt, baking soda and sugar and add to mayonnaise mixture. Mix well. Roll into 1" balls. Place on ungreased cookie sheets. Press down lightly on cookies and sprinkle with sugar. Bake at 400 degrees F for 10 to 12 minutes.

Yield: 4 1/2 dozen

Frosted Sugar Cookies

1 cup powdered sugar
1/2 cup margarine, melted
1/2 cup butter, melted
1 egg
1 teaspoon vanilla
1 teaspoon cream of tartar
1 teaspoon baking soda
1/2 teaspoon salt
2 cups flour

Cream together sugar, margarine and butter. Add egg and vanilla; mix well. Mix together the cream of tartar, baking soda, salt and flour; mix well with butter mixture. Roll into small balls. Flatten with a glass. Bake at 350 degrees F for 10 to 12 minutes.

Frosting:

1/3 cup butter
2 cups powdered sugar
1 egg yolk
1 1/2 teaspoons vanilla
2 tablespoons milk

Mix all ingredients together and frost cool cookies.

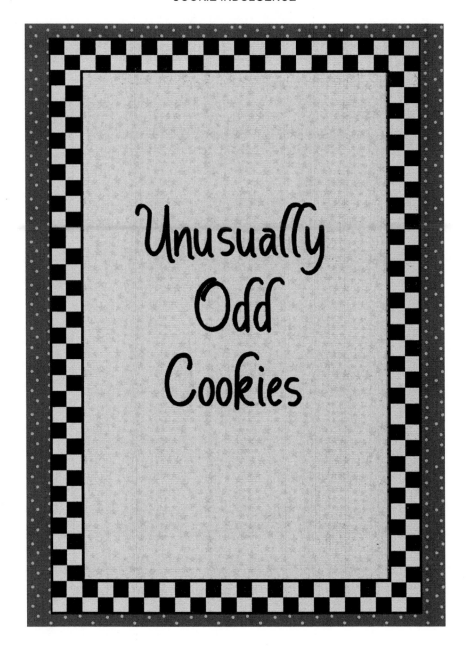

Unusually
Odd
Cookies

Unusually Odd Cookies

Potato Chip Cookies

2 cups butter, melted
1 cup sugar
3 cups flour
2 cups crushed potato chips
1 cup chopped pecans
1 teaspoon vanilla
Powdered sugar

Mix butter and sugar and beat until light and fluffy. Stir in flour and mix well. Stir in potato chips, pecans and vanilla. Drop by spoonfuls on ungreased cookie sheet. Bake in 325 degrees F oven 20 minutes. Sprinkle with confectioners' sugar.

Yield: 7 dozen

Breakfast Bacon Cookies

1/2 cup butter, melted
3/4 cup sugar
1 egg
1/4 teaspoon baking soda
1 cup flour
10 strips of bacon
1/2 cup raisins
2 cups cornflakes

Preheat oven to 350 degrees F. Mix the butter and sugar together. Beat in egg. Add baking soda and flour; mix well. Cook and crumble the bacon, or use the fully cooked bacon and crumble it. Stir the bacon, raisins and cornflakes into the batter. Drop by rounded spoonfuls onto an ungreased cookie sheet. Bake for 15 to 18 minutes or until lightly browned. Store leftovers in refrigerator.

Black Bean Brownies

1 can black beans, 15.5 ounces
3 eggs
2 teaspoons vanilla
3/4 cup white sugar
1/4 cup cocoa powder
2 teaspoons instant coffee
3 tablespoons vegetable oil
1 teaspoon baking powder
1/8 teaspoon salt
1/2 cup milk chocolate chips

Preheat oven to 350 degrees F. Rinse and drain the black beans. In a blender, put the black beans, eggs, vanilla, sugar, cocoa powder, coffee, oil, baking powder and salt; blend until smooth. Pour the batter into a lightly greased 8x8 inch baking dish. Sprinkle the chocolate chips on top of the batter. Bake for 30 minutes or until the sides begin to pull away from the pan.

Pork and Bean Bars

Bar:

1 can pork and beans, drained (16 ounces)
1 can crushed pineapple, drained (8 ounces)
2 cups white sugar
1 cup vegetable oil
4 eggs
2 teaspoons baking soda
2 teaspoons cinnamon
2 cups flour

Preheat oven to 350 degrees F. Mash beans and pineapple with fork and set aside. Mix together sugar, oil, eggs, soda, cinnamon, and flour. Mix well, then add beans and pineapple mixture. Pour into greased 11 x 17" jelly roll pan. Bake for 40 to 45 minutes.

Cream Cheese Frosting:

1/2 cup butter, melted
1 package cream cheese, softened (8 ounces)
1 teaspoon vanilla
2 1/2 cups powdered sugar

Cream together butter, cream cheese and vanilla. Add powdered sugar slowly. Frost cooled bars.

Chinese Noodle Cookies

1 can Chinese crispy Chow Mein noodles (5 oz. can)
2 cups butterscotch chips
1/2 cup peanut butter
2 cups mini marshmallows

Melt in saucepan butterscotch chips and peanut butter; remove from heat. Stir in marshmallows and noodles. Mix and coat well. Drop by spoonful onto wax paper. Let cool about 1 hour.

Chocolate Reindeer Droppings

3 cups quick oats
1 cup coconut
2 cups sugar
1/2 cup butter
1/3 cup cocoa
1/2 cup milk

In a pan, boil sugar, butter, cocoa and milk. Remove from heat and add in the oats and coconut. Mix well and drop by spoonfuls on wax paper. Refrigerate.

Christmas Cookies

No Egg Christmas Balls

1 cup butter
2 teaspoons vanilla
2 teaspoons water
1/3 cup sugar
2 cups flour
1 cup chopped pecans
Red and green sugar

Cream butter and vanilla; add sugar and mix until light and fluffy. Add the water. Stir in the flour and mix well. Add the pecans. Form into 1" balls and roll the balls in the red and green sugar. Bake at 325 degrees F for 20 minutes.

Yield: 3 dozen

Holiday Cookies

1 cup butter
1 cup powdered sugar
1 egg
1 teaspoon vanilla
2 1/2 cups flour
1 cup pecans, chopped
1/2 cup red cherries
1/2 cup green cherries

Cream butter and sugar; add egg and vanilla then flour. Cut up cherries and nuts and add to mixture. Form into long rolls. Chill until firm. Slice and bake 350 degrees F for 10 to 12 minutes.

Christmas Cookies

3/4 cup butter
1 cup sugar
3 ounces red cherries
1 ring of red pineapple diced
1 egg, separated
1 ring green pineapple diced
1 cup walnuts chopped
1 cup flour
1/8 teaspoon salt

Cream butter, sugar and egg yolk until very creamy. Blend in chopped fruit and nuts. Add flour and salt gradually and mix well. Beat egg white stiffly, but not dry. Fold into mixture. Drop by spoonfuls on ungreased cookie sheet. Bake at 350 degrees F about 15 minutes.

Yield: 5 dozen

Cherry Drops

1 cup butter, melted
1 cup confectioner's sugar
2 3/4 cups flour
2 teaspoons baking powder
1/8 teaspoon salt
2 eggs
1 teaspoon vanilla
2 tablespoons milk
Red and green candied cherries

Preheat oven to 375 degrees F. In a bowl, cream the sugar and butter together. Add the eggs and mix well. Beat in the vanilla and the milk. Mix together the flour, salt and baking powder and mix into the batter.

Drop by spoonfuls on an ungreased cookie sheet. Add a cherry in the center of each cookie. Bake for 10 minutes.

Roll Out Cookies

1 cup butter
1 1/2 cups sugar
2 eggs
1 tablespoon vanilla
3 cups flour
2 teaspoons baking powder
1/2 teaspoon salt

Cream together sugar and butter. Beat in vanilla and eggs. Combine flour, baking powder and salt and add to creamed mixture. Roll out and cut shapes with cookie cutter. Bake on ungreased cookie sheet for 6 to 8 minutes at 350 degrees F.

Yield: 2 dozen

Fruitcake Cookies

1 cup butter, melted
1 cup brown sugar, packed
3 cups flour
1/2 cup milk
3 eggs
1 teaspoon baking soda
1 teaspoon cinnamon
2 cups dates, chopped
7 cups pecans, chopped
1 box white raisins
6 slices candied pineapple, chopped
1 cup candied red cherries, chopped
1 cup candied green cherries, chopped

Preheat oven to 300 degrees F. Cream butter and sugar. Add eggs and beat well. In separate bowl, combine flour, baking soda and cinnamon. Add to butter mixture alternately with milk, mixing well after each addition. Stir fruit and nuts into dough, mixing well. Drop by heaping teaspoons onto well-greased cookie sheets. Bake for about 20 minutes.

Yield: 6 dozen

Molasses Krinkles

1 cup brown sugar
3/4 cup butter
1 egg, beaten
4 tablespoons dark molasses
2 1/4 cups flour
2 teaspoons baking soda
1/2 teaspoon cloves
1 teaspoon cinnamon
1 teaspoon ginger
1/4 teaspoon salt

Cream butter and sugar. Add egg and molasses. Add flour, baking soda, cloves, cinnamon, ginger and salt. Roll into balls. Roll balls in white sugar. Place on ungreased cookie sheets. Bake at 350 degrees F for 8 to 10 minutes.

Chocolate-Fruit Christmas Cookies

2 eggs
3/4 cups sugar
2 squares of unsweetened chocolate
4 tablespoons butter
1 cup flour
1/2 teaspoon salt
1/2 teaspoon baking powder
1/2 teaspoon vanilla
1/2 cup each: chopped walnuts, seedless raisins, candied cherries
1/4 cup candied pineapple

In a bowl, beat eggs and sugar. Melt chocolate squares and butter in microwave. Pour the melted chocolate and butter into the mixing bowl. Then add flour, salt, baking powder and vanilla. Mix well. Add nuts, raisins, cherries and pineapple to mixture.

Drop by spoonfuls onto greased cookie sheet. Bake for 10 minutes at 350 degrees F.

Yield: 3 dozen

Cookie
Frostings

Cookie Frostings

Never Fail Caramel Frosting

1 cup brown sugar
5 tablespoons butter
1/4 cup milk
1 cup powdered sugar

In a pan, cook butter and brown sugar until melted. Add the milk. Cook for 3 minutes. Cool. Add 1 cup powdered sugar or enough for right consistency to spread.

Fudge Frosting

1 cup white sugar
1/4 cup spry
1/3 cup milk
2 tablespoons cocoa

Put all ingredients in a saucepan and heat over medium heat, stirring constantly. When you have a rolling boil, time for 1 minute only. Remove and beat until creamy, about 5 minutes, until it cools. (Frosts a 9 x 13 inch cake.)

Butter Cream Frosting

1/4 cup butter
3 tablespoons flour
3/4 cup milk
1 1/2 teaspoons vanilla
1/2 cup butter
3/4 cup sugar

Melt 1/4 cup butter over low heat. Blend in flour and milk. Cook, stirring constantly, until mixture comes to boiling. Cool and add vanilla. Cream 1/2 cup butter and sugar thoroughly and add cooled milk mixture. Beat about 5 minutes. (Will frost tops and sides of two 9" layers.)

German Coconut Pecan Frosting

1 cup sugar
1/2 cup butter
1 teaspoon vanilla
3 egg yolks
1 cup evaporated milk
1 1/3 cups coconut
1 cup pecans, chopped

In a pan, combine sugar, butter, vanilla, egg yolks, and milk. Cook and continuously stir over medium heat about 10 minutes until thick. Add coconut and nuts. Great on brownies.

Cream Cheese Frosting

1 3 oz. package of cream cheese
1/2 cup butter
3 cups powdered sugar
1 teaspoon vanilla
Milk

Combine all ingredients, beat well and add enough milk to make a smooth thick paste.

Easy Penuche Frosting

1 cup brown sugar, packed
1/2 cup butter
2 cups confectioner's sugar
1/4 cup milk

Melt the butter in a pan and add brown sugar. Bring to a boil and cook over low heat for two minutes, stirring constantly. Add milk and bring to boil again. Add confectioner's sugar slowly. Mix the frosting until it's thick enough to spread. If too thick, add hot water.

Ginger Cookies

Gingersnaps

3/4 cup butter
1 cup sugar
1 egg, beaten
2 1/2 cups flour
2 teaspoons baking soda
1 teaspoon cinnamon
1/2 teaspoon ginger
1/2 teaspoon cloves
5 tablespoons molasses

Cream together the butter and sugar. Add the egg and molasses. Add the flour, baking soda, cinnamon, ginger and cloves, and mix well. Make into 1" balls (optional: roll each ball in sugar) and press flat. Bake at 350 degrees F for about 10 minutes.

Refrigerator Ginger Cookies

1 cup sugar
1 cup butter
1/2 cup molasses
2 eggs
4 1/2 cups flour
1 teaspoon ginger
1 teaspoon baking soda
1 teaspoon salt

Cream butter and sugar; add eggs and molasses. Add flour, ginger, baking soda and salt. Shape into rolls and refrigerate several hours. Slice and bake in 350 degrees F oven. Can also be used with cookie cutters. Frost when cool.

Frosting

1/2 cup butter
Powdered sugar
Milk

Brown the butter in small pan. Add powdered sugar and a little milk to the right consistency. Add food coloring, if desired.

Refrigerator Ginger Cookies

Butterscotch Gingerbread Cookies

1 cup butter
1 1/2 cups brown sugar
1 egg
1/3 cup molasses
3 cups flour
2 teaspoons baking soda
1 1/2 teaspoons cinnamon
1 1/2 teaspoons ground ginger
3/4 teaspoon ground cloves
1/2 teaspoon salt
2 cups butterscotch chips

Preheat oven to 350 degrees F. Cream the butter and brown sugar. Add the egg and mix well. Add the molasses. In a separate bowl, mix flour, baking soda, cinnamon, ginger, cloves and salt. Add dry ingredients gradually to the creamed mixture. Stir in the butterscotch chips. Drop by spoonfuls on ungreased cookie sheet and bake for about 9 to 11 minutes.

Gingerbread Filling

2 3 oz. packages cream cheese
1/4 cup milk
1 cup dates, chopped
1/2 cup nuts, chopped

Mix all ingredients together. Use as frosting or spread between layers of gingerbread.

Country Raisin Gingersnaps

1 1/2 cups raisins
3/4 cup butter
1 egg
1 cup sugar
1/4 cup molasses
2 1/4 cups flour
2 teaspoons baking soda
1 teaspoon salt
1/4 teaspoon cloves
1 teaspoon ginger
1/2 teaspoon cinnamon

Chop raisins. Beat together butter, egg and sugar. Blend in molasses. Add flour, baking soda, salt, cloves, ginger and cinnamon. Stir in raisins. Chill. Shape into small balls and roll in sugar. Place on lightly greased cookie sheets. Bake at 375 degrees F for 8 to 10 minutes.

Yield: 3 dozen

Miscellaneous Cookies

Miscellaneous Cookies

Rice Krispies Cookies

1 cup butter
3/4 cup white sugar
1 teaspoon baking soda
2 cups flour
1 teaspoon vanilla
1/2 cup chocolate chips
1/2 cup chopped nuts
2 cups Rice Krispies®

Cream together butter and sugar. Add vanilla. Add flour and baking soda. Mix in the chocolate chips, nuts and Rice Krispies. Drop by spoonfuls onto ungreased cookie sheet and flatten slightly with fork. Bake in 325 degrees F oven for 12 to 13 minutes. Cookies should not brown.

Yield: 5 dozen

Best Chocolate Cookies

2 tablespoons butter
1 1/2 cups of chocolate chips
1 cup flour
1 can sweetened condensed milk
1 cup pecans

Melt butter and chocolate chips in microwave. Mix with flour, sweetened condensed milk and pecans.

Drop on greased cookie sheet and flatten a little. Bake exactly 10 minutes at 325 degrees F.

Coconut Cookies

1 cup butter
1/2 cup brown sugar
1/2 cup white sugar
1 egg
1 cup coconut
1 teaspoon vanilla
2 cups flour
1/2 teaspoon salt
1 teaspoon baking powder
1 teaspoon cream of tartar
1 teaspoon baking soda

Mix butter, sugars, vanilla and egg. Add flour, salt, baking powder, cream of tartar and baking soda. Then add the coconut. Bake at 375 degrees F for 10 to 12 minutes.

Melting Moments

1 cup butter
1/3 cup powdered sugar
2/3 cups cornstarch
1 cup flour

Cream together butter and sugar, add flour and cornstarch. Roll into small balls. Flatten slightly with finger. Bake 10 minutes at 375 degrees F.

Frosting:

1 teaspoon butter
2 teaspoons hot cream or milk
1 cup powdered sugar
1/2 teaspoon vanilla

Brown butter in pan and remove from heat. Add hot cream or milk, powdered sugar and vanilla. Mix and frost cooled cookies.

Low Cholesterol Cookies

1/2 cup margarine
1/2 cup salad oil
1 cup sugar
1 egg
2 1/2 cup flour
1/2 teaspoon salt
1/2 teaspoon baking soda
1 teaspoon cream of tartar
2 teaspoon vanilla

Cream sugar and margarine; add salad oil and egg. Mix rest of ingredients together. Chill 1 hour. Mix into balls, dip in sugar and flatten with greased glass. Bake at 350° until light brown, approximately 9 minutes.

Macaroons

2 egg whites
1 cup coconut
2 cups corn flakes
1 cup sugar
1 teaspoon vanilla

Beat egg whites until stiff; and slowly add the sugar, beating constantly. Fold in vanilla, corn flakes and coconut. Drop by teaspoon on cookie sheet. Bake at 350 degrees F for 15 minutes.

Nutty Coconut Cookies

2 eggs, beaten
1 cup butter
1 teaspoon vanilla
1 cup brown sugar
1 cup white sugar
2 cups flour
1 teaspoon salt
1 teaspoon baking soda
1 cup Rice Krispies
1 cup coconut
1/2 cup oats
1/2 cup nuts

Beat together eggs, butter, vanilla and sugars. In another bowl, mix together flour, salt and baking soda. Add Rice Krispies, coconut, oats and nuts. Add to the butter mixture. Drop on greased cookie sheet and bake in a 350 degrees F oven for 15 minutes.

Coconut Drops

1 cup coconut
2 cups sugar
2 cups butter
3 cups flour
1 cup chocolate chips
1/2 teaspoon salt
1 teaspoon baking soda
1 teaspoon baking powder
1 cup chopped almonds

Cream sugar and butter. Add all the rest of the ingredients and mix well. Make into balls and put on ungreased cookie sheet. Bake at 300 degrees F for 20 minutes.

Pumpkin Cookies

1 cup butter
1 cup sugar
1 can pumpkin
1 teaspoon vanilla
1 egg
2 cups flour
1 teaspoon baking powder
1/2 teaspoon salt
1 teaspoon baking soda
1/2 cup nuts
1/2 cup dates

Cream butter with sugar. Add pumpkin, vanilla and egg and mix well. Mix together flour, baking powder, salt and baking soda. Add to mixture. Add nuts and dates. Drop by spoonfuls onto greased cookie sheet. Bake at 375 degrees F for 8 to 10 minutes.

Frosting:

3 teaspoons butter
4 teaspoons milk
1/2 cup brown sugar
1 cup powdered sugar
1 teaspoon vanilla

Combine butter, milk, brown sugar in small pan cook for 2 minutes, cool. Stir in powdered sugar and vanilla. Spread on cooled cookies.

Grandma's Swedish Cookies

1 cup butter
1/2 cup powdered sugar
1 3/4 cups flour
1 cup chopped pecans
1 teaspoon vanilla

Cream butter. Add sugar slowly. Then add flour, nuts and vanilla. Chill. Roll in small balls and pat down to size on cookie sheet. Bake about 12 minutes at 350 degrees F. When done, roll in powdered sugar.

M&M Cookies

1 cup sugar
1 cup powdered sugar
1 cup oil
4 cups flour
1 teaspoon baking soda
1 cup butter
2 teaspoons vanilla
2 eggs
Pinch of salt
2 cups M&M's®

Mix all ingredients until well blended. Add M&M's®. Drop by spoonfuls on cookie sheet. Bake 8 to 10 minutes at 375 degrees F.

Brown-Eyed Susans

2 cups flour
1 cup butter, melted
3 tablespoons sugar
1 teaspoon almond extract
1/2 teaspoon salt

Preheat oven to 400 degrees. Cream the butter then add sugar, almond extract, salt and flour. Roll spoonfuls of the mixture into balls. Place balls on a greased cookie sheet and flatten slightly. Bake for 10 to 12 minutes.

Frosting:

1 cup powdered sugar
2 tablespoons cocoa
1/2 teaspoon vanilla
2 tablespoons hot water
Almond halves

Combine the sugar and cocoa. Add the water and vanilla. Frost with 1/2 teaspoon of frosting and an almond half.

Yield: 3 dozen

Cream Cheese Cookies

1/2 cup butter, melted
2 packages of 3 oz. cream cheese
2 3/4 cups flour
1 1/2 cups brown sugar, packed
2 tablespoons milk
1 teaspoon salt
1 teaspoon vanilla
1/2 teaspoon baking soda
2 eggs
1 cup pecans, chopped

Heat the oven to 375 degrees F. Mix cream cheese and butter. Stir in the rest of the ingredients. Drop the dough by rounded spoonfuls onto ungreased cookie sheet. Bake for 8 to 10 minutes.

Yield: 6 dozen

Caramel Filled Snicker Doodles

1/2 cup butter
3/4 cup sugar
1 egg
1 1/2 cups flour
1 teaspoon baking powder
1/2 teaspoon baking soda
1/2 teaspoon nutmeg
1/4 teaspoon salt
2 tablespoons sugar
2 teaspoons cinnamon
2 dozen Hershey's Rolo® caramels

Cream butter and sugar. Add egg; beat until fluffy. Blend in flour, baking powder, baking soda, nutmeg and salt to make stiff dough. Shape into 1" balls. Cut or pull each ball apart and insert an unwrapped Rolo® in the center. Put the cookie back together.

Mix 2 tablespoons sugar and 2 teaspoons cinnamon in a small bowl. Roll cookies in sugar mixture. Place on greased cookie sheet. Flatten with fork. Bake at 400 degrees F for 10 to 12 minutes.

Brownies

Coffee Blend Brownies

2 1/2 cups brown sugar, packed
3/4 cup butter
2 teaspoons strong instant coffee
1 teaspoon hot water
2 eggs
2 teaspoons vanilla
2 cups flour
2 teaspoons baking powder
1/2 teaspoon salt
1 cup pecans, chopped
1 cup chocolate chips

Melt brown sugar and butter over low heat until melted.
Dissolve coffee in hot water and stir into butter mixture and
cool. Beat in eggs and vanilla. Mix flour, baking powder and
salt and stir into butter mixture. Add pecans and chips.
Spread in 9x13" pan. Bake at 350 degrees F for 30 minutes.

Yield: 2 dozen

Easy No Bake Brownies

1/2 cup powdered sugar
2 cups semi-sweet chocolate chips
1 cup evaporated milk
1 teaspoon vanilla
4 cups graham cracker crumbs
1 cup walnuts, chopped

Combine cracker crumbs, nuts and sugar in large bowl. Melt chocolate chips in the evaporated milk over low heat; stir constantly. Add vanilla. Reserve 1/2 cup of chocolate mixture and stir crumb mixture into remaining chocolate mixture. Spread in buttered 9x9" pan. Spread the remaining 1/2 cup chocolate mixture over the top. Chill.

Yield: 2 1/2 dozen

Brownie Cookies

1/2 cup butter
1/2 cup sugar (plus extra for dipping at end)
1 egg
1/2 teaspoon vanilla
1/4 teaspoon salt
1 ounce chocolate (Nestle Choco-Bake®) or 1 square
unsweetened baking chocolate
1 cup flour
1 cup chopped walnuts

Cream butter and sugar. Add egg; mix well. Add vanilla, salt, and chocolate. Add flour, then nuts. Drop by teaspoons (first dipped in sugar) onto greased cookie sheet. Bake at 350 degrees F 8 to10 minutes.

Chewy Light Brownies

2 cups brown sugar
1/2 cup butter
1 1/2 cups flour
2 teaspoons vanilla flavoring
2 eggs
1/2 cup nuts

Mix all ingredients together and spread into a greased 8 x 12 inch pan. Bake at 350 degrees F for 30 to 35 minutes.

Cheesecake Mint Brownies

1 package fudge brownie mix (22 ounces)
8 ounces cream cheese, softened
14 ounce can condensed milk
1/2 teaspoon peppermint extract
2 eggs
1 can ready-to-use chocolate frosting

Preheat oven to 350 degrees F. Grease a 9x13 inch cake pan. Make the brownie mix by following the directions written on the package. Pour brownie mix into the cake pan and bake for 15 minutes.

Beat the cream cheese in a large mixing bowl until it becomes fluffy. Add the condensed milk and beat until it is smooth. Stir in the peppermint extract and eggs and mix well.

Pour the mixture over the brownies in the pan and bake for 25 minutes. Allow the brownies to cool and spread them with the ready to use frosting.

Best Brownies

2 1/2 squares chocolate
1 cup butter
4 eggs, beaten
1 cup brown sugar
1 cup white sugar
1 teaspoon vanilla
1 cup flour
1 teaspoon baking powder
1/2 teaspoon salt
1 cup nuts

Melt chocolate and butter together in microwave. Cool somewhat and add eggs and vanilla. Add brown and white sugar. Mix the flour, baking powder and salt; add to chocolate mixture. Add nuts. Bake at 350 degrees F for 40 to 45 minutes.

Graham Cracker Brownies

6 oz. semi-sweet chocolate chips
2 cups graham cracker crumbs
1 14 ounce can sweetened condensed milk
1 teaspoon baking powder

Preheat oven to 350 degrees F. In a bowl, combine cracker crumbs, chocolate chips, milk, and baking powder. Spread into a greased 8x8" baking pan. Bake for 30 to 35 minutes or until toothpick inserted in center comes out clean.

Marshmallow Brownies

1/2 cup butter
1 cup butterscotch chips
3/4 cup brown sugar
2 eggs, beaten
1 1/4 cup flour
1/2 teaspoon salt
2 teaspoons baking powder
1 teaspoon vanilla extract
2 cups mini marshmallows
2 cups chocolate chips

Preheat oven to 350 degrees F. Melt the butterscotch chips and butter in a saucepan and remove from heat. Add the brown sugar and the eggs. Mix together the flour, salt, and baking powder and then add the flour mixture to the melted mixture. Add vanilla.

Let cool for 20 minutes (or put in fridge for less time). It should be cool enough so the chocolate chips do not melt in the mixture. When cool, stir in the marshmallows and the chocolate chips. Put in greased 9x13" pan and bake for 20 to 25 minutes.

Chocolate Cherry Brownies

1 package Pillsbury® Devil's Food cake mix
1 can of cherry pie filling (21 ounce)
1 teaspoon almond extract
2 eggs, beaten

Preheat oven to 350 degrees F and grease and flour jelly roll pan. In large bowl, combine all ingredients and mix well. Pour into pan and bake 20 to 30 minutes.

Frosting:

1/3 cup milk
5 teaspoons butter
1 cup sugar
1 cup semi-sweet chocolate pieces

In a saucepan, combine milk, butter and sugar. Boil 1 minute, stirring constantly. Remove from heat and add chocolate chips. Beat until smooth and pour over warm bars.

Frosted Brownies

1 cup sugar
1/2 cup butter
1 cup flour
4 eggs
1 large can chocolate syrup
1 teaspoon vanilla
1/8 teaspoon salt
Optional – 1/2 cup nuts

Mix all ingredients together. Bake 20 to 25 minutes in a jelly roll pan at 350 degrees F.

Frosting:

1 1/2 cups powdered sugar
6 teaspoons butter
6 teaspoons milk
1 teaspoon vanilla
1 cup chocolate chips

Combine powdered sugar, butter, milk and vanilla in a pan and boil for 1 minute.

For chocolate frosting, stir in chocolate chips. Mix well.

For swirled chocolate frosting, melt the chocolate chips in the microwave. Frost the brownie, then drizzle chocolate on the frosting and using a spoon, make half circle swirl designs to blend.

Frosted Brownies

Muffin Brownies

3/4 cup semi-sweet chocolate chips
1 cup butter
1 cup flour
1 3/4 cups sugar
4 eggs, beaten
1 teaspoon vanilla
1 1/2 cups chopped pecans

Melt chocolate and butter over medium low heat or in microwave. Let cool, then stir in flour, sugar, eggs and vanilla. Stir in nuts. Spoon batter into paper lined or greased muffin tins. Bake at 325 degrees F about 30 minutes or until wooden pick inserted in the center comes out clean.

Coconut Brownies

1 cup butter
1 1/3 cups sugar
3 eggs
1/2 teaspoon salt
1 cup flour
1 square chocolate, melted
3 tablespoons cocoa
1 cup nuts chopped
1/2 teaspoon vanilla

Mix all ingredients above together. Put in ungreased 9x13 inch glass dish. Bake 20 minutes at 375 degrees F.

Topping:

8 ounces shredded coconut
1 can sweetened condensed milk
Can of chocolate frosting

While still warm put shredded coconut on top. Add the can of sweetened milk on top of coconut. Put under broiler until coconut browns (about 15 seconds). Cool. Frost with the can of chocolate frosting.

Chocolate Date Brownies

1 1/2 cups chopped dates (8 oz. package)

Place in 1 cup water and heat to boiling point. Cool.

1 cup sugar
1 cup butter
1 teaspoon vanilla
1 3/4 cups flour
1/2 teaspoon baking soda
1/2 teaspoon salt
3/4 cup cocoa
Chocolate chips
Nuts, chopped

Cream sugar, butter and vanilla. Add flour, baking soda, salt and cocoa. Mix well. Add cooled dates. Put in a greased 9 x 13" pan. Top with chocolate chips and nuts. Bake in oven at 375 degrees F for 25 minutes.

Double Chocolate Brownies

3/4 cup flour
1/4 teaspoon salt
1/4 teaspoon baking soda
1/3 cup butter
3/4 cup sugar
2 tablespoons water
2 cups chocolate chips
1 teaspoon vanilla
2 eggs
1/2 cup chopped nuts

In small bowl, combine flour, salt and baking soda. In saucepan, combine sugar, butter and water. Bring to a boil. Remove from heat. Add 1 cup chocolate chips and vanilla. Beat until smooth. Add eggs one at a time, mixing after each one. Stir in flour mixture and mix well. Add the rest of the chocolate chips and nuts. Spread in greased 9 x 13 inch pan and bake at 325 degrees F for 30 to 35 minutes.

Bar Cookies

Bar Cookies

Yummy Layer Bars

1/2 cup butter
1 cup graham cracker crumbs
1 cup coconut
1 cup semi-sweet chocolate chips
1 cup butterscotch chips
Sweetened condensed milk (14 oz. can)
1 1/2 cup chopped walnuts

Preheat oven to 350 degrees F. Melt butter and put it in a 9x13" pan. Add the remaining ingredients one at a time in order of above so it has seven layers. Bake for 25 to 30 minutes.

No-Bake Peanut Butter Bars

2 cups graham crackers, crushed
1 cup butter, melted
1 cup peanut butter
3 1/2 cups powdered sugar
1 cup chocolate chips

Mix together the graham crackers, butter, peanut butter, and powdered sugar until creamy. Press into a 9x13" pan. Frost with melted chocolate chips (melt in microwave). Refrigerate to set the chocolate and cut into bars.

Carrot Bars

2 jars carrot baby food
2 eggs
1 cup sugar
3/4 cup butter
1 teaspoon vanilla
1 teaspoon cinnamon
1 1/4 cups flour
1 teaspoon salt
1 teaspoon baking soda

Cream together eggs, sugar and butter. Add vanilla and carrots; mix well. Mix in the cinnamon, flour, salt and baking soda. Pour into greased 9x13" pan. Bake at 350 degrees F for 20 to 25 minutes.

Date Bars

1 cup butter, melted
1 cup brown sugar
1 1/2 cups flour
1 1/2 cups quick oats
1 teaspoon baking soda
1 teaspoon salt

Filling:

20 ounces or 1 pound pitted dates
1 cup water
1 cup white sugar
1 cup walnuts, pieces

Preheat oven to 350 degrees F. Mix butter, brown sugar, flour, oats, baking soda and salt together. Pat half of this mixture into 10x13" pan.

Mix the filling ingredients together in a pan. Cook until thick, then cool. Place filling over mixture in pan. Add rest of mix over top of date filling. Bake for 30 minutes or until golden brown.

Lemon Squares

1 cup butter
2 cups flour
1/2 teaspoon salt
1/2 teaspoon baking powder
1/2 cup powdered sugar
4 eggs
6 teaspoons lemon juice
1 1/2 cups sugar
6 teaspoons flour

Mix butter, flour, salt and powdered sugar. Put into a greased 9x13" pan. Bake at 350 degrees F for 15 minutes. Mix eggs, lemon juice, 6 tablespoons flour, baking powder and sugar. Pour the lemon juice mixture over the baked crust. Bake 25 minutes, then sprinkle with powdered sugar.

Nut Goodie Bars

2 cups butterscotch chips
2 cups chocolate chips
1 cup peanut butter
1 1/2 cups miniature marshmallows
1/2 cup salted peanuts

Melt the butterscotch chips and chocolate chips together in a microwave. Add peanut butter, marshmallows and peanuts. Stir all together and put in 9 x 13" greased pan.

Too Easy Orange Bars

2 cups flour
2 cups sugar
2 eggs
2 teaspoons baking soda
2 small cans mandarin oranges, drained
1 teaspoon salt

Mix all ingredients together. Spread in a 9x13" greased pan. Bake at 350 degrees F for 35 minutes. Let cool for 5 minutes.

Glaze:

1 1/2 cups brown sugar
6 tablespoons cream
6 tablespoons butter

Meanwhile for the glaze, cook until melted: brown sugar, cream and butter. Poke holes all over cake and pour glaze over the top. Great with a little Cool Whip or ice cream.

No Bake Chocolate Crunch Bars

1 cup Karo corn syrup
1 cup sugar
6 cups Rice Krispies
1 cup peanut butter
1 cup butterscotch chips
1 cup chocolate chips

Mix the syrup and sugar in a saucepan. Cook over medium heat, stirring until it begins to boil. Remove pan from heat. Add the peanut butter to the pan. Mix in the Rice Krispies. Press the mix into a buttered or greased 9 x 13" pan. In a microwave, melt the chocolate and butterscotch chips. Spread on top of bars.

Chewiest Granola Bars

1 cup brown sugar
1/2 cup butter, melted
1/2 cup light corn syrup
2/3 cups peanut butter
3 cups quick oats
2 teaspoons vanilla
1/3 cup wheat germ
1/2 cup sunflower seeds
1/2 cup raisins or dried cherries
1 cup nuts, chopped

Preheat oven to 350 degrees F. Cream together sugar, corn syrup and butter. Mix in peanut butter, vanilla, sunflower seeds, oats, wheat germ, raisins or dried cherries and nuts. Press into a 9x13" pan. Bake for 15 to 20 minutes.

Ten Dollar Bars

1 cup peanut butter
1 cup butter
2 cups crushed graham crackers
2 cups powdered sugar
2 cups chocolate chips

Combine peanut butter, butter, graham crackers and powdered sugar. Press into buttered 9 x 13" pan. Melt chips in microwave and spread over the top. Chill before cutting and serving.

Caramel Cake Bars

1 package German chocolate cake mix
3/4 cup butter, melted
2/3 cup evaporated milk, separated
2 1/2 cups chocolate chips
1 cup walnuts, chopped
50 Kraft caramels

Mix the cake mix, butter and 1/3 cup milk and put 1/2 of mixture on bottom of a slightly greased 9x13" pan. Bake for 6 minutes at 350 degrees F.

Sprinkle the chocolate chips and walnuts over the baked mixture. In microwave, melt caramels in the other 1/3 cup of evaporated milk. Drizzle this mixture over the chips and nuts. Then spread the rest of the chocolate cake mix on top and bake for 20 minutes.

Nut Variety Bars

1 1/2 cups flour
1 teaspoon salt
3/4 cup brown sugar
1/2 cup butter
1 cup butterscotch chips
2 teaspoons butter
1/2 cup white corn syrup
2 cups mixed nuts

Combine the flour, salt and brown sugar. Cut in the 1/2 cup butter thoroughly and press mixture in a 9x13" pan. Bake at 350 degrees F for 10 minutes; cool. Melt chips, 2 teaspoons of butter and the corn syrup over low heat or in microwave. Spread nuts over cooled baked crust and pour melted chips mixture over the nuts. Bake 10 minutes more at 350 degrees F.

Chocolate Oatmeal Bars

1 cup flour
1 cup butter
1/2 cup brown sugar
1/2 cup white sugar
1/2 teaspoon cinnamon
1 1/2 teaspoons vanilla
1 egg
1 1/4 cups oats
3/4 cup walnuts, divided
2 cups chocolate chips, divided

Combine all ingredients except half of the chocolate chips and nuts. Bake in a 9x13" pan at 350 degrees F for 22 to 28 minutes. Immediately sprinkle remaining chocolate chips and nuts on top.

Toffee Bars

1 cup butter, melted
1 cup brown sugar, packed
1 teaspoon vanilla
1 egg yolk
2 cups flour
1/4 teaspoon salt
1/2 cup chopped nuts
Hershey® bars or milk chocolate chips

Heat oven to 350 degrees F. Grease a 9 x 13" baking pan.
Mix butter, sugar, vanilla and egg yolk thoroughly. Mix in salt
and flour. Press evenly in bottom of pan. Bake 25 to 30
minutes until light brown. The crust will be soft. Remove from
oven and immediately place separated pieces of Hershey
bars on the crust. When chocolate has softened, spread
evenly over crust. Sprinkle with finely chopped nuts.

Butterscotch Squares

1 cup butter, melted
1 cup brown sugar
1 cup white sugar
2 eggs beaten
1 1/2 cups flour
2 teaspoons baking powder
2 teaspoons vanilla
Pecans or walnuts

Mix melted butter, brown sugar and white sugar together. Mix in eggs, flour, baking powder and vanilla. Cover bottom of 9 x 13" greased pan with nuts. Pour mixture over nuts and bake at 350 degrees F for 20 to 30 minutes. Can be sprinkled with powdered sugar.

Honey of A Bar

1/2 cup plus 2 tablespoons honey
3/4 cup creamy peanut butter
2 cups granola
1/2 cup chopped walnuts or peanuts
1 cup rolled oats
1/2 cup sunflower seeds
1 cups chopped raisins or dried apricots
2 eggs, beaten
2 cups crisp rice cereal

Blend the honey and peanut butter in a saucepan and melt over low heat. Remove from heat and allow the mixture to cool. Meanwhile, combine granola, walnuts, oats, sunflower seeds and raisins in a large mixing bowl. Add the peanut butter mixture to the bowl. Stir in the eggs followed by the rice cereal. Press the entire mixture into the bottom of a 9x13" pan. Bake at 325 degrees F 20 to 30 minutes, until edges are golden brown.

Chocolate Glazed Bar Cookies

1/2 cup butter
1/2 cup brown sugar, packed
1 teaspoon vanilla
1 egg
1 1/2 cup flour
1 cup wheat germ
1/2 cup semi-sweet chocolate chips

Beat butter and sugar together. Add vanilla and egg. Stir in flour and wheat germ. Press into 8x8" pan. Bake at 325 degrees F until lightly browned for about 20 minutes. Remove from oven and immediately sprinkle top of bars with chocolate chips. When chocolate has softened, spread carefully over surface with spatula.

Yield: 18 bars

Baby Nathan Bars

1 1/2 cups peanut butter
1 cup light Karo® corn syrup
1 cup sugar
6 cups crisp rice cereal
1 cup chocolate chips
1 cup butterscotch chips

Grease bottom of a 9x13 inch cake pan and set aside. Measure cereal into a large mixing bowl and set aside. Combine peanut butter, corn syrup and sugar in a large saucepan and stir over low heat until smooth. Be sure to stir constantly to avoid burning the mixture.

Pour syrup mixture over cereal and mix through. Pat into the cake pan and sprinkle the surface with the chocolate and butterscotch chips. Heat the bars in the oven or microwave just until chips have melted enough to spread easily over bars.

Corn Flake Peanut Bars

1 cup sugar
1 cup Karo® corn syrup
1/2 cup butter
1 cup peanut butter
1 cup salted peanuts
7 cups corn flakes

Boil the sugar, corn syrup and butter in a saucepan for 1 minute. Stir in the peanut butter until melted. Using a large bowl, mix all ingredients together. Put in a greased 9x13 inch pan. May frost with chocolate frosting, if desired.

Peach Bars

1 1/2 cups flour
1 1/1 cup butter
1/2 cup confectioners' sugar
3 eggs
1 1/4 cups sugar
1/3 cup flour
1 teaspoon vanilla
1/2 teaspoon salt
1 teaspoon baking powder
3 cups sliced fresh peaches

Mix flour, butter and sugar for crust and pat into 9x13 inch pan. Bake 15 minutes at 350 degrees F. Mix remaining ingredients and pour over baked crust. Return pan to oven and bake at 350 degrees F for 35 minutes. Serve with whipping cream.

Fruit Cocktail Bars

1 1/4 cups flour
1/4 teaspoon salt
1 teaspoon baking soda
1/2 teaspoon baking powder
1 can fruit cocktail and juice
Vanilla
1 egg

Topping:

1 1/2 cups brown sugar
Vanilla
2 tablespoons butter
1/2 cup nuts

Combine all ingredients except egg and topping ingredients. Beat well; then add egg. Pour into 13x9 inch pan. Mix all topping ingredients together. Sprinkle topping over bars. Bake 40 to 45 minutes at 350 degrees F.

Blueberry Bars

1/4 cup butter, melted
3/4 cup sugar
1 egg
1/2 cup milk
2 cups flour
1/2 teaspoon salt
2 teaspoons baking powder
2 cups blueberries

Topping:

1/3 cup flour
1/2 cup sugar
1/4 cup butter, melted
1/2 teaspoon cinnamon

Mix sugar, butter and egg. Stir in milk. Mix the flour, baking powder and salt together and add to mixture. Wash and drain the blueberries well. Carefully blend in blueberries. Mix together the topping ingredients. Sprinkle over blueberry mixture. Bake in greased and floured 9 x 9" pan at 375 degrees F for 45 to 50 minutes.

Apple Squares

1 cup quick oats
1/2 cup brown sugar
1 cup flour
1/2 teaspoon salt
1/2 teaspoon baking soda
1/2 teaspoon cinnamon
1/2 cup butter
2 1/2 cups sliced apples
2 tablespoons butter
1/2 cup walnuts
1/4 cup white sugar

Preheat oven to 350 degrees F. Grease the bottom of an 8 or 9 inch baking pan and set aside. In a large bowl, mix together the oats, brown sugar, flour, baking soda, salt and cinnamon. Cut in the butter until the mixture is of a crumbly texture. Evenly spread half of this crumble mixture in the bottom of the baking dish.

Dot the surface with the 2 tablespoons of butter and then evenly spread the sliced apples in the baking dish. Sprinkle the top with walnuts and the white sugar. Finish by topping it off with the remaining half of the crumble mixture. Bake for 40 to 45 minutes.

Chocolate Chip Bars

1/2 cup butter
3/4 cup brown sugar, packed
1 egg, beaten
1/2 teaspoon salt
1/2 teaspoon baking soda
1 1/4 cups flour
1 teaspoon vanilla
1 cup semi-sweet chocolate chips
1/2 cup chopped walnuts

Cream together butter and sugar. Add egg. Stir in salt, baking soda and flour.

Add vanilla and mix. Fold in chocolate and nuts. Spread in greased 15 x 10 inch pan (this will be a thin layer of batter). Bake in 375 degree oven 12 to 15 minutes.

Other books by Bonnie Scott

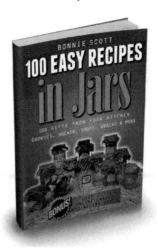

100 Easy Recipes In Jars

100 Easy Camping Recipes

Now in Paperback and Kindle versions

Made in the USA
Middletown, DE
07 February 2015